The United Nations
Leadership and Challenges in a Global World

Antiterrorism Policy
and Fighting Fear

The United Nations:
Leadership and Challenges in a Global World

TITLE LIST

The United Nations
Leadership and Challenges
in a Global World

Antiterrorism Policy
and Fighting Fear

Heather Docalavich

SERIES ADVISOR
Bruce Russett

Mason Crest Publishers
Philadelphia

Mason Crest
450 Parkway Drive, Suite D
Broomall, PA 19008
www.masoncrest.com

Printed and bound in the United States of America.

First printing
9 8 7 6 5 4 3 2 1

Series ISBN: 978-1-4222-3427-3
ISBN: 978-1-4222-3428-0
ebook ISBN: 978-1-4222-8542-8

Library of Congress Cataloging-in-Publication Data
on file

Design by Sherry Williams and Tilman Reitzle, Oxygen Design Group.
Cover photos: Fotolia/Nobilior (top); Dreamstime/Luckydoor (bottom).

CONTENTS

KEY ICONS TO LOOK FOR:

Words to Understand: These words with their easy-to-understand definitions will increase the reader's understanding of the text, while building vocabulary skills.

Sidebars: This boxed material within the main text allows readers to build knowledge, gain insights, explore possibilities, and broaden their perspectives by weaving together additional information to provide realistic and holistic perspectives.

Research Projects: Readers are pointed toward areas of further inquiry connected to each chapter. Suggestions are provided for projects that encourage deeper research and analysis.

Text-Dependent Questions: These questions send the reader back to the text for more careful attention to the evidence presented there.

Series Glossary of Key Terms: This back-of-the-book glossary contains terminology used throughout the series. Words found here increase the reader's ability to read and comprehend higher-level books and articles in this field.

INTRODUCTION

by Dr. Bruce Russett

T HE UNITED NATIONS WAS FOUNDED IN 1945 by the victors of World War II. They hoped the new organization could learn from the mistakes of the League of Nations that followed World War I—and prevent another war.

The United Nations has not been able to bring worldwide peace; that would be an unrealistic hope. But it has contributed in important ways to the world's experience of more than sixty years without a new world war. Despite its flaws, the United Nations has contributed to peace.

Like any big organization, the United Nations is composed of many separate units with different jobs. These units make three different kinds of contributions. The most obvious to students in North America and other democracies are those that can have a direct and immediate impact for peace.

Especially prominent is the Security Council, which is the only UN unit that can authorize the use of military force against countries and can require all UN members to cooperate in isolating an aggressor country's economy. In the Security Council, each of the big powers—Britain, China, France, Russia, and the United States—can veto any proposed action. That's because the founders of United Nations recognized that if the Council tried to take any military action against the strong opposition of a big power it would result in war. As a result, the United Nations was often sidelined during the Cold War era. Since the end of the Cold War in 1990, however, the Council has authorized many military actions, some directed against specific aggressors but most intended as more neutral peacekeeping efforts. Most of its peacekeeping efforts have been to end civil wars rather than wars between countries. Not all have succeeded, but many have. The United Nations Secretary-General also has had an important role in mediating some conflicts.

UN units that promote trade and economic development make a different kind of contribution. Some help to establish free markets for greater prosperity, or like the UN Development Programme, provide economic and technical assistance to reduce poverty in poor countries. Some are especially concerned with environmental problems or health issues. For example, the World Health Organization and UNICEF deserve great credit for eliminating the deadly disease of smallpox from the world. Poor countries especially support the United Nations for this reason. Since many wars, within and between countries, stem from economic deprivation, these efforts make an important indirect contribution to peace.

Still other units make a third contribution: they promote human rights. The High Commission for Refugees, for example, has worked to ease the distress of millions of refugees who have fled their countries to escape from war and political persecution. A special unit of the Secretary-General's office has supervised and assisted free elections in more than ninety countries. It tries to establish stable and democratic governments in newly independent countries or in countries where the people have defeated a dictatorial government. Other units promote the rights of women, children, and religious and ethnic minorities. The General Assembly provides a useful setting for debate on these and other issues.

These three kinds of action—to end violence, to reduce poverty, and to promote social and political justice—all make a contribution to peace. True peace requires all three, working together.

The UN does not always succeed: like individuals, it makes mistakes . . . and it often learns from its mistakes. Despite the United Nations' occasional stumbles, over the years it has grown and moved for-ward. These books will show you how.

The Twitter hashtag #BringBackOurGirls on a Paris street in October of 2014 in response to the kidnapping of 276 girls by the terrorist group Boko Haram in Chibok, Nigeria, in April of the same year.

CHAPTER ONE

An Overview of the UN Approach to Terrorism

From the earliest days of recorded history, humankind has perpetrated acts of terror on their fellow beings in hopes of **demoralizing** and frightening each other. The word zealot, now used to describe anyone who is fanatical about a particular philosophy or cause, originally applied to an ancient Jewish group that worked to expel the Romans from Judea through the use of terrorist techniques.

WORDS TO UNDERSTAND

accomplice: someone associated with another person, usually in wrongdoing.

conventions: agreements between countries, less formal than treaties.

demoralizing: discouraging, creating a loss of confidence.

gunrunning: trafficking in guns and ammunition.

protocols: established procedures often formulated and signed by diplomatic negotiators.

unilaterally: done with input from only one side of an issue.

To send Rome a message that they were not wanted, the Zealots would attack Roman officials in broad daylight—and in front of large groups of onlookers. Many other words are now used to describe terrorists or criminals. The word *assassin*, from an ancient Muslim society that attacked leaders who deviated from strict Muslim law, and *thug*, from the Thugees, a Hindu sect that preyed on British travelers in India, actually have their roots in terrorist actions.

This painting by Francesco Hayez depicts the destruction of the Second Temple in Jerusalem during the First Jewish-Roman War. Simon bar Giora, a revolutionary leader of the Zealots, led a major role during this battle.

Terrorism in a Modern Context

Terrorist activity affects virtually every corner of today's world. As a result, individual governments and regional and international governing bodies have been forced to address the issue.

Terrorism was first formally addressed by the League of Nations, the predecessor of the modern United Nations. In 1937, the League of Nations drafted the Geneva Convention for the Prevention and Punishment of Terrorism. This was intended to be a vehicle by which member nations would be able to follow a consistent plan to address the underlying causes of international terrorism and to identify, try, and punish terrorists.

Despite the good intentions of the League of Nations, its plan was never widely adopted. For the next several years, individual nations **unilaterally** addressed terrorist incidents. In the decades that followed, the UN was formed and grew into an international body of true importance with some power to enforce its resolutions.

DEFINING TERRORISM

The definition of terrorism is the act of causing fear, through violence or the threat of violence, to create political pressure on a group or government. However, member countries of the United Nations have found it difficult to agree on a single definition of terrorism.

Development of Current Conventions on Terrorism

Despite the growth and increasing influence of the UN, it did not address the issue of terrorism until 1963. What emerged was a series of fourteen **conventions** that dealt with international terrorism from legal and political perspectives. Instead of crafting one document to identify a single policy on terrorist activity of all types, the twelve individual conventions were drafted over a period of years as new threats were identified.

All fourteen conventions have common features. Each one defines a particular type of terrorist violence as a crime under the convention, such

The 1960s and 1970s saw several terrorist acts committed against commercial airlines. The Montreal Convention of 1971 defined terrorism in the skies and addressed this type of violence against civilian targets.

as hijacking an airplane. Each convention requires individual member countries to criminalize terrorist acts in its own domestic laws. Every one of the conventions also identifies certain policies by which the involved parties are required to establish jurisdiction over the crime, and the country where the suspect is found is obligated to establish jurisdiction over the crime in question. That country is then required to refer the crime for international prosecution if the country does not extradite the suspect. This requirement is commonly known as the principle of "no safe haven for terrorists." Most nations believe it is vital to deprive terrorist suspects of havens where they can flee and be safe from prosecution.

Although the fourteen major conventions and **protocols** related to a country's responsibilities for combating terrorism would seem to provide ample protection from terrorist activity, the evening news confirm terrorist acts still occur around the world. These laws are sometimes ineffective because many countries are not yet party to these legal instruments, or they have not started to enforce them. Some believe the conventions do not go far enough in identifying terrorist crimes and appropriate means of prosecution.

The following identifies the fourteen major terrorism conventions and provides a brief summary of each.

Convention on Offenses and Certain Other Acts Committed on Board Aircraft

This is also referred to as the Tokyo Convention of 1963, a convention that applies to terrorist acts affecting airline safety. If necessary to protect the safety of the aircraft, the law authorizes the pilot to impose reasonable measures, including restraint, on any person the pilot has reason to believe has committed or is about to commit a crime. The law also requires member states to take custody of offenders and to return control of the aircraft to the pilot or an authorized representative.

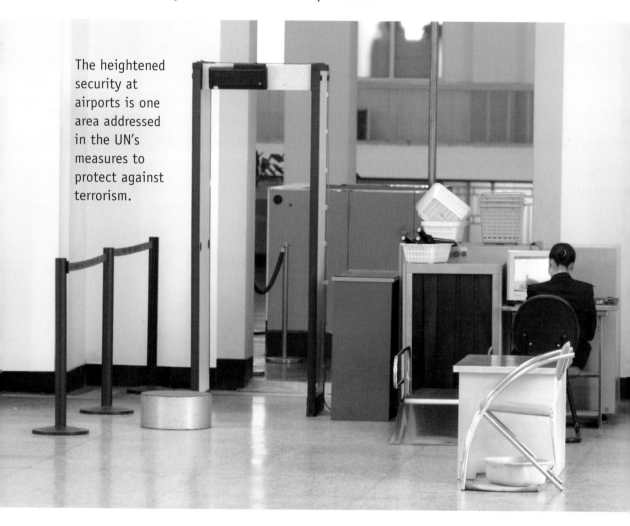

The heightened security at airports is one area addressed in the UN's measures to protect against terrorism.

Convention for the Suppression of Unlawful Seizure of Aircraft

Also known as the Hague Convention of 1970, this law makes it a crime for any person on board an aircraft in flight to "unlawfully, by force or threat thereof, or any other form of intimidation [to] seize or exercise control of that aircraft" or to attempt to do so. The law requires parties to the convention to make hijackings punishable by "severe penalties." It also requires countries that have custody of offenders to either extradite the offender or submit the case for prosecution. Countries are required to assist each other in connection with criminal trials brought under the convention.

Convention for the Suppression of Unlawful Acts Against the Safety of Civil Aviation

The Montreal Convention of 1971 applies to acts of aviation sabotage, such as bombings aboard aircraft in flight. The convention makes it a crime for any person to intentionally perform an act of violence against a person on board an aircraft in flight, if that act is likely to endanger the safety of that aircraft, to place an explosive device on an aircraft, or to attempt such acts. It is also unlawful to be an **accomplice** to a person who performs

SECURITY COUNCIL TAKES THE LEAD

Since 2001, the Security Council has adopted many resolutions regarding terrorism. Several of these resolutions condemn various acts of terror. These resolutions include:

2001 Condemnation of September 11 attacks against United States

2002 Condemnation of hostage taking in Moscow
Condemnation of terrorist attacks in Kenya

2003 Condemnation of bombings in Istanbul
Condemnation of bomb attack in Bogota, Colombia

2004 Condemnation of bomb attacks in Madrid

2005 Condemnation of terrorist attacks in Iraq
Condemnation of terrorist attacks in London

or attempts to perform such acts. The convention requires countries that are parties to the convention to make such crimes punishable by "severe penalties." Countries that have custody of offenders must either extradite the offenders or submit the case for prosecution, and countries are required to assist each other in connection with criminal trials brought under the convention.

Convention on the Prevention and Punishment of Crimes Against Internationally Protected Persons

Passed in 1973, this law outlaws attacks on senior government officials and diplomats. The convention defines internationally protected persons as a head of state, a minister for foreign affairs, or a representative or an official of a state or international organization. The law requires each country to criminalize and make punishable "by appropriate penalties which take into account heir grave nature," the intentional murder, kidnapping, or other attack on an internationally protected person, a violent attack on official premises, private accommodations, or the means of transport of such a person. It is also a crime to threaten or attempt to commit such an attack or commit any act "constituting participation as an accomplice."

International Convention Against the Taking of Hostages

The Hostages Convention of 1979 is very straightforward: any person who seizes or detains and threatens to kill, to injure, or to continue to detain another person in order to compel a third party, namely, a state, an international intergovernmental organization, a natural or juridical person, or a group of persons, to do or abstain from doing any act as an explicit or implicit condition for the release of the hostage commits the offense of taking of hostage within the meaning of this convention. In recent years, especially with the 2014 rise of ISIS, or the Islamic State, the terrorist group operating in northern Iraq and Syria, many hostages are held for ransom, to help finance terrorist activities. As with the other conventions, a state that is a party to the convention must criminalize hostage taking and provide for the apprehension and prosecution of hostage takers.

Convention on the Physical Protection of Nuclear Material

The Nuclear Materials Convention of 1980 combats the unlawful theft and use of nuclear material. It criminalizes the unlawful possession, use, and transfer of nuclear material; the theft of nuclear material; and threats to use nuclear material to cause death or serious injury to any person or substantial property damage.

Protocol for the Suppression of Unlawful Acts of Violence at Airports Serving International Civil Aviation

Written in 1988 as a supplementary to the Convention for the Suppression of Unlawful Acts Against the Safety of Civil Aviation, this measure extends and supplements the provisions of the earlier Montreal Convention to include all terrorist acts at airports serving international civil aviation.

Terrorism affects innocent people in all regions of the world. In March 2005, terrorists in Lashwa Juwayn, Afghanistan, kidnapped six workers of the Watan Kar Construction Company and burned or stole all of the company's equipment.

As Iraq was withdrawing from Kuwait following its loss in the 1990–1991 Persian Gulf War, it set Kuwait's oil wells on fire, as shown in this image taken from a U.S. fighter plane taking part in flyovers. Some have argued that the deliberate destruction of the oil fields was an act of terrorism, even though it occurred during wartime.

Convention for the Suppression of Unlawful Acts Against the Safety of Maritime Navigation

Also written in 1988, this convention applies to terrorist activities on ships and establishes a legal framework to prosecute acts against international shipping. Under this law, it is a crime for a person to seize or exercise control over a ship by force, threat, or intimidation; to perform an act of violence against a person on board a ship if that act is likely to endanger the safe navigation of the ship; or to place a destructive device or substance aboard a ship.

Protocol for the Suppression of Unlawful Acts Against the Safety of Fixed Platforms Located on the Continental Shelf

Drafted in 1988, this document applies to terrorist activities on fixed offshore platforms, like those used to drill for oil. Its legal guidelines are similar to those for terrorist acts against aircraft and ships.

The plastic explosive P.E.4 pictured here was used by British military to destroy bombs in a controlled explosion in 2006 in Afghanistan. The UN convention on plastic explosives aims to make such material detectable and therefore less likely to be used in a terrorist attack.

Convention on the Marking of Plastic Explosives for the Purpose of Detection

This provision was negotiated in 1991 in response to the 1988 bombing of Pan Am Flight 103.This convention allows chemical marking to facilitate detection of plastic explosives as a means to combat aircraft sabotage. The law is designed to control and limit the use of unmarked and unde- tectable plastic explosives, and parties to the convention are obligated in their respective countries to ensure effective control over "unmarked" plastic explosives. Unmarked explosives are those that do not contain one of the detection agents described in the Technical Annex that ac- companies the treaty.

International Convention for the Suppression of Terrorist Bombing

Created by a UN General Assembly Resolution in 1997, this convention establishes a framework for international jurisdiction over the unlawful and intentional use of explosives and other lethal devices against various defined public places with intent to kill or cause serious bodily injury, or with intent to cause extensive destruction of the public place.

International Convention for the Suppression of the Financing of Terrorism

Drafted in 1999, this convention requires countries to take measures to prevent the direct or indirect financing of terrorists. This also applies to those groups claiming to have charitable, social, or cultural goals that engage in such illicit activities as drug trafficking or **gunrunning**. The law requires states to hold liable those who finance terrorism for such acts; and provides for the identification, freezing, and seizure of money allocated for terrorist activities, as well as for the return of the forfeited funds to other states on a case-by-case basis.

ATTACKS AGAINST THE UN

UN peacekeepers and employees are often victims of terrorist attacks. Such was the case on October 3, 2014, when nine UN peacekeepers in the African nation of Mali were ambushed and killed. The attack on the Nigerian peacekeepers by a group linked to al Qaeda was strongly condemned by the UN Security Council and other nations. The UN mission in Mali began in July 2012. Between that date and 2014, thirty peacekeepers had been murdered and another ninety had been wounded.

Memorial ceremony being held for fallen UN Nigerian peacekeepers in Mali.

International Convention for the Suppression of Acts of Nuclear Terrorism

This 2005 convention covers a broad range of potential terrorism targets, including nuclear power plants. It also encourages nations to cooperate and prevent terrorist attacks on such facilities.

Convention on the Suppression of Unlawful Acts Relating to International Civil Aviation

Drafted in 2010, this convention makes it a crime to use a civilian aircraft as a weapon. Specifically, the convention makes it criminal to use private aircraft to discharge a biological, chemical, or nuclear weapon. It also makes it a crime to transport such weapons and unleash a cyber attack on air navigation facilities.

* * *

In addition to these fourteen conventions, the UN General Assembly and the Security Council have adopted several resolutions pertaining to terrorism. The laws and actions established by the UN regarding international terrorism are broad and often spread across the UN's many branches and agencies. However, the fourteen formal conventions against terrorism provide a basic framework in which member nations can coordinate their antiterrorism activities.

The 2005 UN convention on nuclear terrorist threats seeks to protect nuclear power plants from terrorist attacks. Pictured here is the nuclear plant in Chinon, France, located in the Loire River Valley.

CHAPTER ONE

TEXT-DEPENDENT QUESTIONS

1. How many conventions has the UN approved to combat various forms of terrorism?

2. Name two ancient "terrorist" groups.

3. What was the predecessor of the United Nations?

RESEARCH PROJECTS

1. Research the various terrorist groups in the world today and then plot their locations on a world map.

2. Write a brief report on one of the fourteen international conventions against terrorism and why it was adopted.

The United Nations headquarters in New York City is where the Security Council meets on issues relating to terrorism and other serious security concerns.

CHAPTER TWO

Terrorism and the Security Council

The Security Council is the most powerful branch of the UN. Its purpose is to maintain peace and security among nations. While other bodies of the UN can only make recommendations to member governments, the UN Charter gives the Security Council the power to make decisions member governments must follow. Decisions of the council are known as UN Security Council Resolutions.

 WORDS TO UNDERSTAND

adherence: sticking to a belief or practice.

blocs: groups of countries or political parties with the same goal.

compliance: conforming to a regulation or law.

proliferation: the rapid spread of something.

sustenance: something, especially food, that supports life.

President Barack Obama leads a Security Council meeting at the United Nations headquarters in New York City in September of 2009.

Structure of the Security Council

In order for the Security Council to meet on a moment's notice, a country's representative for each Security Council member must always be present at UN headquarters. The council has five permanent members: the People's Republic of China, France, the Russian Federation, the United Kingdom, and the United States of America. Ten other members are elected by the General Assembly for two-year terms beginning on January 1, with five replaced every year. The members are chosen by regional groups and confirmed by the UN General Assembly. The African, Latin American, and Western European **blocs** select two members each. The Arab, Asian, and Eastern European blocs select one member each. The final council seat alternates between Asian and African selections. As of January 2015, elected members are Angola, Chad, Chile, Jordan, Lithuania, Malaysia, New Zealand, Nigeria, Spain, and Venezuela.

As the only body of the UN with the power to compel individual member states to abide by its resolutions, the Security Council has a critical role in the war against international terrorism. As a result, the Security Council has passed a number of resolutions dealing with terrorism and what individual states must do to cooperate with the UN and other governments in the prevention of terrorist activity, as well as the apprehension, extradition, and prosecution of terrorist suspects.

FACING A CONTINUING THREAT

Although the Security Council has taken real and measurable steps to combat global terrorism, the struggle against this threat is far from over. "Through our collective efforts, we must ensure that all counterterrorism actions and policies are consistent with international human rights and humanitarian laws," UN Secretary-General Ban Ki-moon said in a message to the UN Counter-Terrorism Committee in September 2014.

The terrorist attack on the Pentagon, pictured here, and the World Trade Center on September 11, 2001, led to Resolution 1373.

A Critical Role in the War on Terror: Resolution 1373

In recent years, the Security Council has been very active on matters regarding terrorism. This was spurred, in part, by the need to respond strongly and quickly to the terrorist attacks on New York City and Washington, D.C., as well as the forced downing of an airplane in Pennsylvania on September 11, 2001. These attacks on "9/11" were against the United States but they killed citizens of many different countries and caused worldwide economic damage. Charged with maintaining the world's peace and security, the Security Council felt a need to react in a way that would have a lasting and meaningful effect.

On September 28, 2001, the Security Council adopted Resolution 1373, which declared, "acts, methods and practices of terrorism are contrary to the purposes and principles of the United Nations." It required UN members to "become parties as soon as possible to the relevant international conventions and protocols" and "to increase cooperation and fully implement the relevant international conventions and protocols."

Monitoring Compliance by Member States

Resolution 1373 also established the Counter-Terrorism Committee (CTC) to monitor the implementation of the resolution and increase the capability of members to fight terrorism. The CTC has now become the UN's primary body for cooperative action against international terrorism. The committee consists of one representative from all fifteen members of the Security Council Members of the Security Council elect the committee's chairman and vice chairmen.

Resolution 1373 imposes binding obligations on all member nations, with the aim of combating all forms of terrorism. The resolution requires that members deny all forms of financial support to terrorist groups; prevent the possibility of safe haven, **sustenance**, or support for terrorists; share information with other governments on any groups who have committed or are planning terrorist acts; cooperate with other governments in the investigation, detection, arrest, and prosecution of those involved in such acts; criminalize active and passive assistance for terrorism in domestic laws and bring violators of these laws to justice; and become party as soon as possible to the relevant international conventions and protocols relating to terrorism. The CTC demands that every member take specific actions to meet the requirements of the resolution based on the unique circumstances in each country. UN members must report to the CTC regularly to show the changes and progress their countries are making to contribute to the global war against terrorism.

All reports received by the CTC are assessed by one of three sub-committees. As part of the review process, each member nation is invited

Turkish Foreign Minister Ahmet Davutoglu and U.S. Secretary of State Hilary Clinton launch the Global Counterterrorism Forum in New York City in September of 2011. The Forum is part of the international community's efforts to support the UN's fight against terrorism.

to have a representative attend part of the subcommittee's discussion of the report. Independent advisers give the subcommittees technical advice. These advisers support the work of the CTC with expertise in the fields of legislative drafting, financial law and practice, customs law and practice, immigration law and practice, extradition law and practice, police and law enforcement, and illegal arms and drug trafficking. The subcommittees can also obtain additional technical assistance from advisers in other fields.

Based on the analysis of each nation's reports and other available information, the CTC assesses countries' **compliance** with Resolution 1373. The CTC then sends a letter to each nation, including input from any relevant experts. These letters may ask for further information on issues discussed in their reports and other matters the CTC may consider related to the implementation of the resolution. Nations are required to respond to the issues raised in the letter in another report, which is due within three months. Long-term implementation of Resolution 1373 is an ongoing process that consists of three different stages.

UN resolutions must be carried out around the world by UN peacekeeping forces.

Stage A

In the first stage, the CTC is concerned with whether a nation has in place effective counterterrorism legislation in all areas of activity related to Resolution 1373. Specific attention is paid to financial support of terrorists. Legislation is viewed as a key issue, because without an efficient legal framework, member nations cannot develop effective means to prevent terrorism, or bring terrorists and their supporters to justice. Reviews of a country's reports will continue to focus on Stage A until the CTC has no further comments about the goals of this stage.

Stage B

This stage begins once countries have legislation in place addressing all aspects of Resolution 1373. During this phase of the resolution, a nation strengthens its governmental machinery to enforce Resolution 1373-related legislation. This includes activities designed to prevent recruitment

OTHER ACTIVITIES AGAINST TERROR

The UN Security Council has passed several other measures designed to prevent terrorism. Although the CTC remains the primary body reporting to the Security Council on the progress of individual nations in combating the spread of international terrorism, other committees assist in this important work. For example, United Nations Security Council Resolution 1540 was passed on April 28, 2004, creating the 1540 Committee.

This resolution calls on member countries to take additional measures to prevent the **proliferation** of nuclear, chemical, or biological weapons and their means of delivery. The 1540 Committee is charged with evaluating compliance in a similar manner to the way the CTC oversees general **adherence** with antiterrorism measures. The difference between the two bodies is that the 1540 Committee is concerned solely with measuring compliance of nations in adopting stricter methods to control the proliferation of weapons of mass destruction.

Chemical and biological weapons are a major concern in the international community's terrorism prevention program. Pictured here is an Israeli soldier in 2006 during a chemical and biological weapons exercise.

by terrorist groups, limit the movement of terrorists, and eliminate the establishment of terrorist safe havens and any other forms of passive or active support for terrorists or terrorist groups.

To meet the requirements of effective enforcement required by Stage B, a country must have in place police and intelligence structures to detect, monitor, and apprehend those involved in and who support terrorist activities. Countries must demonstrate that customs, immigration, and border controls have been implemented to prevent the movement of terrorists and the establishment of safe havens. Finally, they must demonstrate that controls are in place preventing access to weapons by terrorists.

Stage C

The CTC recognizes that every nation is unique, and the results of these differences in circumstances mean that progress through these priorities will not be uniform. However, the CTC requires all countries show progress toward implementation of Resolution 1373 at the fastest possible speed. Stage C occurs once the CTC determines that a country has met the requirements of the previous stages. Stage C is the monitoring stage, during which the CTC makes certain that countries continue to be in compliance with the requirements.

As a result, the CTC has been meeting with member states to implement counterterrorism policies including holding workshops for judges, prosecutors, and law enforcement personnel. CTC personnel also discuss with member countries the reasons why some individuals become "radicalized" leading them to committing terrorists acts.

The committee also helps nations prosecute terrorism cases while respecting the rule of law. "Even though the terrorist threat has become more diffuse, a strong and fair criminal justice system remains central to a comprehensive counter-terrorism approach," Raimonda Murmokaite, chairwoman of the CTC, told the Security Council in a briefing on May 28, 2014, "[We continue] to engage with member states on ways to develop tailored and more effective judicial responses to emerging trends.

CHAPTER TWO

TEXT-DEPENDENT QUESTIONS

1. Who are the five permanent members of the United Nations Security Council?

2. What does nuclear non-proliferation mean?

3. When did terrorists fly planes into the World Trade Center and Pentagon?

RESEARCH PROJECTS

1. Make a timeline of the current UN secretary-general's public comments on terrorists, noting a specific quote, the date, and the location. Note any other significant details that help give meaning to his statement, such as the event the secretary-general was responding to.

2. One of the images in this chapter is of the inaugural session of the Global Counterterrorism Forum. Research this organization or another non-UN group involved in supporting the UN's goals and activities on counterterrorism.

The Friends of Yemen group meets in September 2012 in New York and aims to support Yemen's efforts against terrorists in the country. Britain, the United States, Saudi Arabia, and Egypt, along with other countries participate, as does the UN. Secretary-General Ban Ki-moon is speaking in the center.

CHAPTER THREE

The UN Role in the Prevention of Terrorism

With a global membership and a commitment to world security, the UN is uniquely positioned to play a crucial role in the international fight against terrorism. Individual members often struggle with internal political, economic, and bureaucratic limitations. As an independent international organization, the UN has more freedom in establishing an antiterrorism agenda.

 WORDS TO UNDERSTAND

disaffected: discontented with authority.

extremist: having to do with radical political or religious beliefs.

imperative: absolutely necessary.

mentorship: act of serving as a guide or tutor.

money laundering: the transferring of illegally obtained money through various businesses and accounts so as to hide it.

ratification: the act of formally approving something.

A UN peacekeeper in the North Kivu province of Pinga in the Democratic Republic of the Congo interacts with the local children in 2013. Defeating terrorism begins with educating those affected most.

A Structure for Preventing Terrorism

The United Nations Office on Drugs and Crime (UNODC) is a critical component of the UN's efforts to prevent terrorism. Headquartered in Vienna, Austria, the UNODC has a drug program and a crime program. The crime program deals with terrorism issues through the Terrorism Prevention Branch (TPB), an agency operating under the guidance of the Division for Treaty Affairs (DTA). The TPB provides technical assistance and advisory services to countries in their fight against terrorism. As a consequence, UNODC's operational activities focus on strengthening legislation against terrorism in individual member countries.

UNODC aims at responding quickly and effectively to requests for counterterrorism assistance, in compliance with the priorities set by the Commission on Crime Prevention and Criminal Justice and the CTC. Types of assistance include reviewing domestic legislation and providing advice on drafting new laws, giving in-depth assistance on the **ratification** and implementation of new legislation against terrorism through **mentorship** programs, and offering training to national criminal justice systems on the practical application of the universal instruments against terrorism.

In carrying out its activities, UNODC works closely with the Counter-Terrorism Committee, and an efficient working relationship has developed between the two agencies. The CTC receives and analyzes the reports received from member countries and arranges technical assistance for those in need of aid. The TPB provides this assistance. Regular contact with the CTC is maintained by sharing information and identifying with the CTC countries most in need of legislative aid. In this way, the CTC is able to direct requests for assistance from the needy countries to UNODC.

Achieving Results

The benefits of this cooperation can be seen in the progress the TPB has made. It has worked to educate lawmakers and criminal justice officials from dozens of countries on the provisions of Security Council Resolution

TERRORIST—OR FREEDOM FIGHTER?

George Washington was a terrorist, true or false? Osama bin Ladin was a terrorist, true or false? It depends on whom you ask. After all, both used violence to attack an established government.

A February 2002 Harris Poll, found most Americans consider acts of violence against dictatorial, military, or undemocratic governments to be the work of freedom fighters. Violence against other, nonoppressive governments are deemed acts of terrorism by the majority of Americans.

George Washington led the American colonists against the British. For this, he came to be known as a founding father of the United States. According to the British, however, he was a rebel bent on seizing control of their colonies in North America.

1373, and on the requirements for ratifying and implementing the universal antiterrorism instruments and international cooperation arrangements.

National action plans have been developed together with individual governments as a means of setting clear and achievable goals related to terrorism prevention. Special legislative drafting committees have been established to study the provisions of the instruments and to make recommendations to governments regarding ratification, as well as the practical realization of the proposed legislation.

By 2014, the TPB had field experts working in Central and Southeast Asia, East and West Africa, Latin America, and the Middle East and North Africa. In each of those regions, experts provide help in counterterrorism activities, each tailored to the regional political, legal, and institutional specificities of each country. The TPB holds specialized workshops to give countries from the same region a forum in which to compare progress, learn from each

The United Nations provides human resources—experts and other professionals—to nations around the world for training and support purposes.

other, and harmonize legislative efforts. These workshops have produced final documents focusing on the follow-up technical assistance needs of participating countries. The TPB has supplied nations with assistance in completing reports to the CTC. Terrorism prevention experts have been strategically dispatched to a number of critical regions to support and follow up on these assistance activities. The TPB also gives each nation online help to counter terrorism by using interactive tools for training.

Working Partnerships

All ongoing work and all TPB activities are guided and coordinated by the CTC. When appropriate, other UN agencies are consulted. The TPB also draws on existing UNODC internal expertise, such as in the areas of **money laundering** and organized crime and corruption. In addition, the Office of Legal Affairs is also consulted on relevant matters.

The free exchange of expertise and information with other international, regional, and national institutions is an important tool. Some organizations regularly provide assistance to the TPB. These include the Council of Europe, the Intergovernmental Authority on Development, the International Monetary Fund, the Organization of American States, and the Organization for Security and Cooperation in Europe. The TPB expects that partnerships with such organizations will continue to expand in order to allow an efficient response to the needs and requests of members in their terrorism prevention plans.

The UN works with other international organizations in its fight against terrorism, including such regional groups as the Organization of American States, or OAS. Pictured here is the opening ceremony of the OAS's 42nd General Assembly meeting in 2012 in Ecuador.

A Global Strategy to Prevent Terror

In addition to the various committees and bodies created by the UN to guarantee the consistent and universal application of existing resolutions dealing with terrorism, former UN secretary-general, Kofi Annan, unveiled a new global strategy against terrorism on March 10, 2005. Annan outlined his plan in a keynote address to the Closing Plenary of the International Summit on Democracy, Terrorism, and Security. He highlighted several areas the UN still needs to address. The main elements of this comprehensive plan, formally adopted as the "UN Global Counter-Terrorism Strategy" can be summarized by what is now referred to as "the five Ds."

The first "D" comes from "dissuading **disaffected** groups from choosing terrorism as a tactic." Groups often resort to terrorist acts because they think those tactics are effective, and often because they receive approval for their actions from religious and political leaders. Kofi Annan's plan includes applying pressure to ensure all political and moral authorities proclaim terrorism unacceptable. It is also **imperative** that terrorist acts committed to achieve a specific goal—for example, to obtain the release of a prisoner—prove ineffective.

Finally, in accomplishing the first "D," Kofi Annan proposed a measure that many in the international community have been seeking for some time. Citing a report issued by a High-Level Panel on Terrorism, the secretary-general stated:

A DECADE LATER

A decade after the UN implemented Anna's terrorism strategy, Secretary-General Ban Ki-moon acknowledged that many terrorists are crossing borders to take advantage of conflict is such states as Iraq and Syria.

"I have sounded the alarm about the vicious and unjustifiable actions of these groups and the danger they pose to Iraq, Syria, the wider region, and international peace and security," Ki-moon said. "We need a creative and comprehensive political strategy in Syria and beyond to stem the flow of foreign terrorist fighters.

Under Britain's Proceeds of Crime Act (POCA), police in West Midlands, England, seized over £1.3 million (over $1.9 million) thought to have been "earned" from the sale of stolen goods. Local laws such as POCA are important tools used to help police track down criminals, including terrorists.

> The Panel calls for a definition of terrorism which would make it clear that any action constitutes terrorism if it is intended to cause death or serious bodily harm to civilians and noncombatants, with the purpose of intimidating a population or compelling a Government or an international organization to do or abstain from any act. I believe this proposal has clear moral force, and I strongly urge world leaders to unite behind it. Not only political leaders, but civil society and religious leaders should clearly denounce terrorist tactics as criminal and inexcusable.

This is a significant development as the UN has debated an official definition of terrorism for years without reaching a consensus. The second "D" comes from "denying terrorists the means to carry out their attacks."

The fifth "D" under Kofi Annan's strategy to tackle terrorism is "defend human rights." Pictured here is Georgette Gagnon, the director of human rights for UNAMA, the UN Assistance Mission in Afghanistan, in a 2013 meeting with local officials in Jalalabad, Afghanistan.

Although the UN already has many measures in place to prevent the financing of terrorist activities, gaps remain. Provisions outlined in this strategy included taking effective action against money laundering. One way the UN acted on this matter was to adopt the nine Special Recommendations on Terrorist Financing produced by the OECD's Financial Action Task Force.

In addition to denying terrorists funding, it is critical to not allow them access to nuclear materials. In his remarks, Annan established the link between a nuclear attack and the economic crisis that would inevitably follow. With a major economic crisis, poverty increases and affects things like infant mortality. In other words, regardless of what country sustains the attack, the effects of the attack would be felt around the globe. As a result, Annan urged the UN member countries at the time to universally adopt, without delay, the international convention on nuclear terrorism. Annan's successor, Ban Ki-moon, also urged the importance of eradicating nuclear and other weapons of mass destruction.

The third "D" represents "deter states from supporting terrorist groups." This is easily accomplished by strengthening sanctions and other coercive measures available to the Security Council to encourage nations to stop harboring terrorist groups.

The fourth "D" stands for "develop state capacity to prevent terrorism." As described earlier, the UN has performed a great deal of work in this regard. The CTC and the TPB are working to develop domestic systems in poor nations to protect them from exploitation by terrorist groups. However, Annan identified additional ways the international community could assist the world's poorest nations in resisting terrorist groups and their influence.

The United Nations Development Program and its Electoral Assistance Division have critical roles in assisting with the establishment of stable forms of government. Legitimate and fair elections can be monitored by these bodies, and they have many resources at their disposal to help strengthen young democratic states.

Terrorists with **extremist** philosophies often target uneducated people holding narrow world-views. Therefore, it is necessary the international community promotes the availability of education and a free press in disadvantaged areas of the world. The United Nations Education, Scientific and Cultural Organization (UNESCO) can play a vital role in promoting education and reducing the vulnerability of the general population to distorted ideology in the developing world.

The fifth "D" is for "defend human rights." Annan at the time voiced concern that some policies implemented to combat terror have infringed on individual rights. As a potential solution, the UN Commission on Human Rights adopted a resolution calling on the secretary-general to appoint a special representative who would study the compatibility of counter-terrorism measures with international human rights laws.

In 2008, that representative drew up a framework for such compatibility titled "Protect, Respect, and Remedy." According to the framework, it is the duty of each nation to protect against human rights abuses by third parties, including businesses, "through appropriate policies, regulation, and adjudication." In 2011, the Human Rights Council endorsed a new set of "Guiding Principles for Business and Human Rights" designed to provide a standard for preventing and addressing adverse impacts on human rights by business activity.

* * *

The UN has taken action to prevent terror on many fronts. The accomplishments of the CTC and the TPB have been effective and measurable. New legislation and security measures implemented as a result of these efforts have made it more difficult for terrorist groups to operate in many areas of the world. New strategies outlined by Secretary-General Kofi Annan and implemented by his successor Ban Ki-moon give a clear and organized course of action as the global community continues its important work preventing acts of terror.

CHAPTER THREE

TEXT-DEPENDENT QUESTIONS

1. Describe the job of the UN's Terrorism Prevention Branch.

2. Define money laundering.

3. Summarize the UN's strategy against terrorism outlined by UN Secretary-General Kofi Annan in 2005.

RESEARCH PROJECTS

1. One criticism of the United Nations is that it has yet to agree on a universal definition of terrorism. Break into groups and draft a definition of terrorism. Read and discuss your definition with the rest of the class.

2. Use a map of the world to indicate the locations of terrorist attacks that have occurred over the last ten years.

The aftermath of the terrorist attack on New York City on September 11, 2001, when hijackers from the terrorist group al Qaeda flew two planes into the World Trade Center towers.

CHAPTER FOUR

The United Nations and al Qaeda

The attacks of September 11, 2001, increased public awareness of the al Qaeda terrorist network. However, international justice officials and individual governments had been aware of the threat presented by al Qaeda for years before the devastating attacks. The UN had also dealt with issues pertaining to the terrorist network prior to September 11. To understand current policies pertaining to al Qaeda, one must first understand that organization's long and bloody history.

 WORDS TO UNDERSTAND

coalition: in military terms, a group of nations joined together for a common purpose against a common enemy.

guerrilla: unorganized and small-scale warfare carried out by independent units.

infidel: someone whose beliefs are different in relation to a specific religion.

sanctions: actions agreed upon and taken to persuade countries or other entities to change their policies.

theocracy: a form of government in which religious figures rule in the name of God.

A History of al Qaeda

Al Qaeda is Arabic for "the base," and the organization was founded by a wealthy Saudi businessman named Osama bin Laden in the early 1980s. His initial goal was to support the war in Afghanistan, where Afghan Muslims were fighting to free their country from Soviet occupation. The Muslim victory in Afghanistan fueled the fighters' idea of jihad, a campaign by Muslims in defense of the Islamic faith, sometimes interpreted by some as a demand for armed conflict. Trained fighters called mujahedin, who had gone to Afghanistan to fight against the Soviets, began returning to countries including Egypt, Algeria, and Saudi Arabia. They brought back extensive experience in **guerrilla** warfare and a desire to continue the jihad.

Sometime in 1989, al Qaeda dedicated itself to opposing non-Islamic governments through force and violence. It began to provide training camps and guesthouses in various countries for the use of the organization

and its affiliated groups. With their extreme interpretation of Islam, they recruited young men from all over the world. The organization sought to recruit U.S. citizens who could travel easily throughout the Western world to deliver messages and perform financial transactions for the benefit of al Qaeda and its affiliated groups—and to help carry out operations. By 1990, al Qaeda was providing military and intelligence training for itself and its partners. This training occurred in Afghanistan, Pakistan, and the Sudan.

The United States and many of its allies supported the Afghan mujahedin that fought against Soviet occupation in the 1980s. Seen here are wounded Afghan fighters being transported for donated medical treatment.

JIHAD

When asked to define "jihad," many Americans might say it refers to a violent holy war waged by Muslims against non-Muslims. Although that is one definition, it is not the only one.

A "jihad" is a crusade for principles or a belief. In the context of Islam, it refers to the defense, spread of Islam, and does allow violence for that purpose if it is deemed necessary. But there are also nonviolent ways to defend Islam, such as getting a religious education and writing and speaking to promote Islam.

There is a third type of jihad, the "inner jihad," also called the "Greater Jihad." This jihad refers to each Muslim's internal struggle for "spiritual self-control."

Al Qaeda's initial objective was to drive U.S. armed forces out of Saudi Arabia and Somalia by any means necessary. Members of al Qaeda issued fatwahs, special statements on Islamic law, indicating such attacks were righteous and necessary. Al Qaeda regards its enemies in the West, including the United States, as **infidel** nations that provide essential support for other infidel nations.

The presence of U.S. armed forces in the Gulf, along with the arrest, conviction, and imprisonment in the United States of al Qaeda members, prompted fatwahs supporting attacks against U.S. interests, domestic and foreign, civilian and military. Those fatwahs resulted in attacks against the United States in locations around the world, including Somalia, Kenya, Tanzania, Yemen, Spain, Great Britain, and the United States.

Both the 1993 and 2001 attacks on the World Trade Center in New York City have been attributed to al Qaeda. Since 1993, thousands of people have died in al Qaeda-provoked attacks around the world. Over the years, al Qaeda has been headquartered in Sudan, Pakistan, and Afghanistan. Several businesses, both legal and illegal, provided income and cover to al Qaeda operatives.

In the years before the attacks of September 11, 2001, al Qaeda was believed to be headquartered in the rural areas of Afghanistan, where the members were given safe haven by the radical Taliban government. The Taliban ruled Afghanistan as a Muslim **theocracy**, and all law in the country was based on a very strict and narrow interpretation of Islam.

Two Afghan boys help turn over the ammunition left behind by the Taliban to a joint U.S.–Afghan operation in Barge Matal, Afghanistan, in July 2009.

UN Action Against al Qaeda

In the wake of a number of terrorist attacks by al Qaeda and its affiliated groups, the UN first dealt specifically with al Qaeda in Security Council Resolution 1267, which was adopted on October 15, 1999. In that document, the Security Council cited concerns about human rights violations in Afghanistan and various other violations of international law by the Taliban government. The document also addressed the obligations of the Taliban government to assist in the extradition and prosecution of al Qaeda members.

The resolution lists a series of failures by the Taliban government to meet its obligations under international law. Many of these related directly to Taliban support of the al Qaeda network. Some of the violations outlined by the Security Council include:

- The sheltering of terrorist in areas controlled by the Taliban.

- Providing safe haven to Osama bin Ladin and allowing him and his associates the ability to operate terrorist training camps.

The resolution declared that these failures by the Taliban government to comply with international law constituted a threat to international peace and security, and listed a series of demands and **sanctions** the Security Council would impose if the Taliban did not comply including:

- The Taliban must ensure that its territory is not used for the sanctuary or training of terrorists or for the planning of terrorist acts.

- The Taliban should cooperate in bringing known terrorists to justice, including turning over Osama bin Laden to authorities for prosecution.

- All countries should assist in bringing bin Laden to justice.

- All countries should deny permission for aircraft owned or operated by the Taliban to take off or land in their territory unless explicitly allowed by the UN for humanitarian reasons.

- All countries should freeze funds owned or controlled by the Taliban and ensure that no funds are made available to the Taliban unless explicitly allowed by the UN for humanitarian reasons.

Although the Security Council made clear demands of the Taliban and outlined specific methods to be used to force the Taliban's compliance, the Security Council was unsuccessful in persuading the Taliban government to change its policies on any issues addressed by Resolution 1267. In 2000, the Security Council passed another resolution, further increasing the sanctions imposed on Afghanistan and freezing the personal assets of Osama bin Laden and his known al Qaeda associates. These sanctions had little effect. Afghanistan continued to provide a safe base from which al Qaeda could carry out its terrorist activities.

No Safe Haven

Following the attacks of September 11, 2001, it was soon obvious to international authorities that al Qaeda was responsible. The UN responded with a series of resolutions that refined and enhanced Resolution 1267 and that were designed specifically to target al Qaeda, to curtail their activities worldwide, and to monitor the progress of member nations in implementing this strategy. Eliminating terrorists safe havens became the international community's top priority. On this basis, the United States, together with other **coalition** nations, eventually took military action against the Taliban government. The UN responded to the attacks with a series of measures designed to increase its power in dealing with all kinds of terrorism.

The Security Council established the 1267 Committee to monitor the implementation by member nations of the sanctions it imposed on individuals and entities related to the Taliban, Osama bin Laden, or al Qaeda. The committee maintains a list of individuals and entities for this purpose. In the twelve resolutions, as of February 2015, that followed 1267, up through Resolution 2161 and 2170 approved in 2014, the Security Council required all member countries to freeze assets of every person and entity on the list. Also, member countries are obligated to prevent anyone on the list from entering or traveling through their countries, and to prevent the direct or indirect supply, sale, or transfer of arms and military equipment to anyone on the list.

U.S. soldier searches the haystack of a suspected terrorist safe house in the Paktika province of Afghanistan in 2007.

THE DEATH OF BIN LADEN

On May 2, 2011, U.S. Special Forces killed Osama bin Laden, who was holed up in a compound in the Pakistani city of Abbottabad. U.S. intelligence identified the compound in August of 2010, and the next month alerted President Barack Obama to that fact. Over the next several months, the United States gathered more intelligence on the site and began taking steps to raid the compound. On April 29, 2011, at 8:20 p.m., President Obama okayed the raid. On May 2, a group of Navy Seals raided the site in two Black Hawk helicopters, and within forty minutes bin Laden was dead, killed by a gunshot wound to his head.

The fight to prevent the growth of the al Qaeda network and to bring those who have been involved with its terrorist acts to justice is the ongoing work of the Security Council and the 1267 Committee. It remains the one of the most important, if not the top, concern of the international community.

By 2014, the UN-sanctioned war against the Taliban in Afghanistan led by the United States was at an end. At the time, President Barak Obama announced that the last American troops in Afghanistan would leave by the end of 2016. Only a token force would remain behind to guard the U.S. embassy in Kabul and to help the Afghans with other security matters.

However, as the United States decreased its military presence in the region, it continued to fight terrorists using unmanned drone strikes, especially in Yemen and Pakistan.

Yazidi refugees find protection in a shelter run by the International Rescue Committee as they flee from the advance of the terrorist group ISIS in northern Iraq in August of 2014.

Afghan Army Lt. Fakhrudin talks with a village elder on a patrol during March of 2012, as part of the effort of coalition forces, led by the United States, to gain the trust of local communities in the fight against the Taliban.

A New Threat

By 2014, a new terrorist threat emerged—ISIS (or ISIL), which stands for the Islamic State in Iraq and Syria (or the Levant). Emerging from both battle-worn areas, ISIS—once an offshoot of al Qaeda, and later a rival faction—was in control, at the end of 2014, of a wide area that stretched across eastern Syria and northern and western Iraq. Its leader was Abu Bakr al-Baghdadi.

The group caught the world's attention by beheading British and American citizens in 2014. The United States and other nations began waging an air war against ISIS in August 2014, following reports that ISIS was close to exterminating the Yazidi Kurdish religious minority in Iraq by killing them unless they converted to Islam. As of early 2015, the U.S.–led air campaign and the ground assaults by Kurdish fighters were making some headway against ISIS, even as the terrorist group committed new atrocities with the beheadings of two Japanese hostages, and the burning of a captured Jordanian pilot alive as they confined him to a cage.

In its statements and actions against al Qaeda, the UN must be careful to distinguish between terrorist organizations and the religion of Islam they claim to represent. Pictured here is a mosque, a Muslim place of worship in the Middle East.

As ISIS rose in prominence in 2014, along with al Qaeda affiliate the al-Nusra Front (ANF), the United Nations aimed to help the international community cripple the group's march across Iraq and Syria. The UN targeted ISIS through the accumulated actions and sanctions approved in the measures based on Resolution 1267, which addressed the terrorist organization al Qaeda and affiliated groups. Its most recent, as of August 2014, is Resolution 2170, which singles out ISIS, the al-Nusra Front, and their leaders as targets of its condemnation, sanctions, and accusations of crimes against humanity. The UN will continue this new fight against terrorism through the work of its agencies, including the Counter-Terrorism Committee (CTC) and the Office on Drugs and Crime (UNODC), the vigilant monitoring by the 1267 Committee, and the power of the international community behind it.

FROM SECURITY COUNCIL RESOLUTION 2170

Approved August 15, 2014

Acting under Chapter VII of the Charter of the United Nations,

1. Deplores and condemns in the strongest terms the terrorist acts of ISIL and its violent extremist ideology, and its continued gross, systematic and widespread abuses of human rights and violations of international humanitarian law;

2. Strongly condemns the indiscriminate killing and deliberate targeting of civilians, numerous atrocities, mass executions and extrajudicial killings, including of soldiers, persecution of individuals and entire communities on the basis of their religion or belief, kidnapping of civilians, forced displacement of members of minority groups, killing and maiming of children, recruitment and use of children, rape and other forms of sexual violence, arbitrary detention, attacks on schools and hospitals, destruction of cultural and religious sites and obstructing the exercise of economic, social and cultural rights, including the right to education, especially in the Syrian governorates of Ar-Raqqah, Deir ez-Zor, Aleppo and Idlib, in northern Iraq, especially in Tamim, Salaheddine and Niniveh Provinces;

3. Recalls that widespread or systematic attacks directed against any civilian populations because of their ethnic or political background, religion or belief may constitute a crime against humanity, emphasizes the need to ensure that ISIL, ANF and all other individuals, groups, undertakings and entities associated with Al-Qaida are held accountable for abuses of human rights and violations of international humanitarian law, urges all parties to prevent such violations and abuses;

4. Demands that ISIL, ANF and all other individuals, groups, undertakings and entities associated with Al-Qaida cease all violence and terrorist acts, and disarm and disband with immediate effect;

5. Urges all States, in accordance with their obligations under resolution 1373 (2001), to cooperate in efforts to find and bring to justice individuals, groups, undertakings and entities associated with Al-Qaida including ISIL and ANF who perpetrate, organize and sponsor terrorist acts and in this regard underlines the importance of regional cooperation;

6. Reiterates its call upon all States to take all measures as may be necessary and appropriate and in accordance with their obligations under international law to counter incitement of terrorist acts motivated by extremism and intolerance perpetrated by individuals or entities associated with ISIL, ANF and Al-Qaida and to prevent the subversion of educational, cultural, and religious institutions by terrorists and their supporters;

From the UN Security Council press release, "Security Council Adopts Resolution 2170 (2014) Condemning Gross, Widespread Abuse of Human Rights by Extremist Groups in Iraq, Syria (http://www. un.org/press/en/2014/sc11520.doc.htm).

CHAPTER FOUR

TEXT-DEPENDENT QUESTIONS

1. When did Osama bin Laden die?

2. Who are the Taliban?

3. Which terrorist group was responsible for the 9/11 attacks?

RESEARCH PROJECTS

1. Compare and contrast al Qaeda and ISIS. Create a chart showing the similarities of and differences between each organization.

2. Write a biography of Osama bin Laden or create a photographic timeline of his life.

This photo was shot soon after the two terrorist bombs exploded during the Boston Marathon in April 2013. Boston-area hospitals were well-equipped to handle the numbers of injuries which helped reduce severe injury and loss of life.

CHAPTER FIVE

In the Aftermath of Terrorism

In addition to the many policies the UN has developed to prevent terrorism, it also has a **mandate** to assist those devastated by the effects of terror. As the world's leading international body, the UN has a unique ability to respond to crises worldwide. The specific kind of assistance it offers is based on the type of attack and the ability of the affected population to cope with the aftermath of an attack.

 WORDS TO UNDERSTAND

debilitating: reducing strength or energy.

disseminate: to spread.

infrastructure: the basic physical structures of a region or state, made up of roads, buildings, and other types of installations.

mandate: an official instruction by an authority.

subsidiary: a group controlled by a larger one.

Emergency Humanitarian Aid

Terrorist attacks have far-reaching effects. In addition to loss of life or destruction of property, often the economy of a country is damaged. In an underdeveloped area of the world, economic devastation can make it impossible to obtain even the most basic necessities. When a country's food supply is endangered, the UN subsidiary World Food Programme (WFP) is often the first line of defense. The WFP is the world's largest humanitarian organization.

Hunger is a consequence of many types of emergencies, including natural disasters like the tsunami tragedy in Asia, to manmade crises such as civil war or major terrorist attacks. Increased civil conflict, war, and natural disasters in the world's poorest nations have caused an explosion in food emergencies. Whatever the cause of an emergency, the WFP is the primary tool of the UN's humanitarian response.

As the threat of large-scale, catastrophic terrorism looms, the WFP has established a new protocol for emergency response that can be applied to a variety of food emergencies. The first step is to conduct an emergency needs assessment to establish whether international food and nonfood assistance is warranted. Often an emergency needs assessment is conducted in conjunction with other UN agencies. This approach to providing aid immediately following a disaster helps ensure that assistance programs are swiftly implemented in the event a terrorist attack disrupts the food or water supply.

The World Food Programme (WFP) in Mali in February 2013, distributing food to refugees displaced by civil war involving al Qaeda factions as well as other groups fighting for control in the North African country.

Japanese self-defense forces unload the chemical boron delivered by the U.S. Air Force on March 19, 2011. The delivery of boron, used to help control the effects of the nuclear melt-down, was part of the international response to the flood that damaged the Fukushima Daiichi nuclear power plant following the earthquake and tsunami.

Responding to a Nuclear or Radiological Attack

In matters relating to atomic energy, the UN relies on its affiliation with the International Atomic Energy Agency (IAEA). In 1986, a twenty-four-hour operational headquarters, the Emergency Response Centre (ERC), was established in Vienna, Austria. The ERC is a central body to which nations and international organizations can promptly and effectively direct initial warnings, advisory messages, requests for emergency assistance, and information.

As the threat of nuclear terrorism has grown over the last few decades, it has become clear that timely and appropriate action in the aftermath of such an attack will be necessary to save as many lives as possible, as well as address the political and social effects of such an act. In June 2004, the IAEA adopted the Action Plan for Strengthening the International Preparedness and Response System for Nuclear and Radiological Emergencies. The plan covers three main areas: international communication, international assistance, and creation of a sustainable infrastructure of preparedness and response to a nuclear or radiological emergency. Following the Triple Disaster in Japan in March 2011, when a giant tsunami damaged the Fukushima Daiichi nuclear power plant, the IAEA began reassessing the 2004 action plan. In September of 2011, it approved the IAEA Action Plan on Nuclear Safety and is expected to issue a full-scale report in September of 2015.

The IAEA also works directly with other international bodies to provide a coordinated international response on as many fronts as

DIRTY BOMBS

So-called dirty bombs are one of the major threats the IAEA faces. Experts fear that terrorists can explode a conventional bomb packed with radioactive materials sometimes used in such benign industries as agriculture and scientific research. The bomb would throw radiation into the environment. Experts say the blast itself from the conventional bomb would be more deadly than any radioactive threat; however, a dirty bomb could cause panic. However, a dirty bomb is not a nuclear bomb, which creates an explosion millions of times more powerful.

possible. The Food and Agriculture Organization of the United Nations (FAO), the World Meteorological Organization (WMO), and the World Health Organization (WHO) are full parties and important partners to the Convention on Early Notification of a Nuclear Accident (CENNA) and the Convention on Assistance in the Case of a Nuclear Accident or Radiological Emergency (CANARE). Individual governments also have their own response programs in place, and the IAEA and these other UN-affiliated groups are working to enhance rather than replace those systems.

Responding to a Biological or Chemical Attack

In today's world of rapidly evolving technology, some scientific advances prove to hold as much threat as benefit. This is especially true when considering the availability of biological and chemical agents to terrorists. Several small attacks of this nature have already occurred as forms of domestic terrorism.

In March 1995, members of a Japanese religious sect named the Aum Shinrikyo (Supreme Truth) placed opened containers of a liquefied form of sarin, a deadly chemical, on five different cars on the Tokyo subway system. Twelve people were killed in that chemical attack; five thousand required medical attention. Anthrax attacks occurred in the United States in 2001, killing five people. The deadly bacteria was grown in a very low-tech environment and transported through the U.S. mail. Although these attacks have been small and domestic in nature, the international community cannot discount the possibility of a large-scale international attack of this type.

The UN has a significant role to play following a biological or chemical attack. Which UN organizations are involved depends on the circumstances of the attack and the population affected. They may include the UN Security Council. As the use or threat of use of chemical or biological weapons clearly constitutes a threat to international peace and security, it will therefore fall within the responsibility of the Security Council to investigate and respond to such attacks.

A U.S. marine from the Chemical Biological Incident Response Force (CBIRF) leads a "victim" out of a simulated subway chemical attack in New York City in April 2010. Training for possible chemical attacks is a crucial part of making preparations for terrorist attacks.

AUM SHINRIKYO

The Japanese cult Aum Shinrikyo was virtually unknown in the West until the sarin attack on the Tokyo subway in 1995. Founded in 1986 by Asahara Shoko, the group was heavily focused on the end of the world.

The attack on the subway system, as well as other violent acts, led to the conviction of Asahara. In 2000, under a new leader, the group changed its name to Aleph, "beginning," and started on a campaign to change its image.

If it is a large-scale attack, the UN can provide humanitarian assistance. The Emergency Relief Coordinator of the United Nations was mandated by the General Assembly in 1992 to serve as the focal point and coordinating official for UN emergency relief operations. The coordinator is also the under secretary-general for Humanitarian Affairs..

Other UN Agencies in the UN Arsenal

A range of UN agencies are critical in the international response to terrorist attacks. Some of the most important are noted below.

The Office for the Coordination of Humanitarian Affairs (OCHA) has established an emergency response system for coordinating actions taken by the international community to deal with natural disasters and environmental emergencies, including terrorist acts. It is responsible for mobilizing and organizing international disaster response and can be contacted on a twenty-four-hour basis in case of a crisis.

The Organization for the Prohibition of Chemical Weapons (OPCW) deals with issues regarding the use of chemical weapons. The assistance available from the OPCW following a chemical attack falls into two categories: hardware (mainly protective equipment) and a variety of assistance teams.

The World Health Organization (WHO) acts as a coordinating agency on all international health issues, especially in emergency situations. The use of chemical or biological weapons on a large scale would likely result

The Organization for the Prohibition of
Chemical Weapons (OPCW), headquartered in
The Hague, Netherlands, provides medical teams
to member nations after a chemical crisis.

in catastrophic public health and medical emergencies, including a sudden and significant increase in the numbers of illnesses and deaths from a variety of diseases. The WHO would play a critical role in responding to any such emergency.

The World Organization on Animal Health (WOAH) and the Food and Agriculture Organization (FAO) would also have important roles to play following a biological or chemical attack. Both organizations are prepared to respond to any emergency affecting crops or livestock, as a chemical or biological attack would likely do.

* * *

The UN has many programs in place to cope effectively with a terrorist attack. However, most of the UN's subsidiary bodies still have plans in progress to upgrade their abilities to respond should disaster strike. The General Assembly and the Security Council work daily on strategies dealing with terrorism-related issues. As those efforts begin to bear fruit, the world's preeminent international body will have a greater ability to prevent terrorism and address its aftereffects.

CHAPTER FIVE

TEXT-DEPENDENT QUESTIONS

1. What is the job of the WFP?

2. What is the role of the International Atomic Energy Agency (IAEA) in response to terrorist attacks?

2. Which terrorist group attacked the Tokyo subway system in 1995?

RESEARCH PROJECT

Research a natural or man-made disaster and how the UN responded to the crisis. What type of assistance was provided? How was this disaster similar to a terrorist attack? Do you think the same kind of emergency response would be effective in the case of a terrorist attack?

TIME LINE

1937 The League of Nations drafts the Geneva Convention for the Prevention and Punishment of Terrorism.

1963 The UN passes the Convention on Offenses and Certain Other Acts Committed On Board Aircraft.

1970 The UN passes the Convention for the Suppression of Unlawful Seizure of Aircraft.

1971 The UN passes the Convention for the Suppression of Unlawful Acts Against the Safety of Civil Aviation.

1973 The UN passes the Convention on the Prevention and Punishment of Crimes Against Internationally Protected Persons.

1979 The UN passes the International Convention Against the Taking of Hostages and the Convention on the Physical Protection of Nuclear Material.

1986 The Emergency Response Centre (ERC) is established in Vienna, Austria.

1988 The UN passes the Protocol for the Suppression of Unlawful Acts of Violence at Airports Serving International Civil Aviation, supplementary to the Convention for the Suppression of Unlawful Acts Against the Safety of Civil Aviation, and the Convention for the Suppression of Unlawful Acts Against the Safety of Maritime Navigation and the Protocol for the Suppression of Unlawful Acts Against the Safety of Fixed Platforms Located on the Continental Shelf.

1991 The UN passes the Convention on the Marking of Plastic Explosives for the Purpose of Detection; the UN General Assembly mandates the Emergency Relief Coordinator of the United Nations to oversee emergency humanitarian aid.

1997 The UN passes the International Convention for the Suppression of Terrorist Bombing and the International Convention for the Suppression of the Financing of Terrorism.

1999 The Security Council adopts resolution 1267, defining the obligations of the Taliban government to assist in the extradition and prosecution of al Qaeda members.

2000 Sanctions against the Taliban are increased as the Afghan government fails to meet the demands of Resolution 1267.

2001 Al Qaeda terrorists attack the United States, and the Security Council adopts Resolution 1373, creating the CTC. The IAEA passes a resolution to develop a plan of action for strengthening the international emergency response for a nuclear accident or terrorist attack.

2004 The Security Council passes Resolution 1535, designed to revitalize the efforts of the CTC and establishes the Counter-Terrorism Committee Executive Directorate. The Security Council passes Resolution 1540.

2005 The UN passes the International Convention for the Suppression of Acts of Nuclear Terrorism.

2011 Osama bin Laden is killed by U.S. Navy Seals at a secret compound in Pakistan.

2014 A terrorist organization called ISIS begins wielding a path of destruction in Syria and Iraq. The UN responds with new extensions of its anti–al Qaeda measures, including Resolution 2161 and Resolution 2170.

FURTHER RESEARCH

Books

Comras, Victor. *Flawed Diplomacy: The United Nations & the War on Terrorism*. Potomac Books, 2010.

Haq al-Ani, Abdul. *Genocide in Iraq: The Case Against the UN Security Council and Member States*. Clarity Press, 2013.

Martin, Gus. *The SAGE Encyclopedia of Terrorism*, 2nd edition. Thousand Oaks, CA: Sage Reference, 2011.

Shanty, Frank. *Counterterrorism: From the Cold War to the War on Terror*. Santa Barbara, CA: Praeger, 2012.

Online Sources

Food and Agriculture Organization of the United Nations: www.fao.org

International Atomic Energy Agency: www.iaea.org/

Organization for the Prohibition of Chemical Weapons: www.opcw.org

UN Counter-Terrorism Committee: http://www.un.org/en/sc/ctc/

United Nations Office for the Coordination of Humanitarian Affairs www.reliefweb.int/ocha_ol/index.html

United Nations Office on Drugs and Crime (UNODOC) http://www.unodc.org/

World Food Program: www.wfp.org

World Health Organization: www.who.int

World Organization for Animal Health (OIE): www.oie.int

NOTE TO EDUCATORS: This book contains both imperial and metric measurements as well as references to global practices and trends in an effort to encourage the student to gain a worldly perspective. We, as publishers, feel it's our role to give young adults the tools they need to thrive in a global society.

SERIES GLOSSARY

abstain: not to vote for or against proposal when a vote is held.

Allies: the countries that fought against Germany in World War I or against the Axis powers in World War II.

ambassador: an official representative of one country to another country.

amendments: process of changing a legal document.

appeal: a formal request to a higher authority requesting a change of a decision.

appeasement: a deliberate attempt pacify a potentially troublesome nation.

arbitration: the process of resolving disputes through an impartial third party.

asylum: protection granted by a nation to someone who has left fled their country as a political refugee.

Axis: the alliance of Germany, Italy, and Japan that fought the allies in World War II.

blocs: groups of countries or political parties with the same goal.

bureaucracy: a complex system of administration, usually of a government or corporation.

capital: material wealth in the form of money or property.

civil law: law of a state dealing with the rights of private citizens.

coalition: in military terms, a group of nations joined together for a common purpose against a common enemy.

codification: the arrangement of laws into a systematic code.

Cold War: a largely nonviolent conflict between capitalist and communist countries following World War II.

compliance: conforming to a regulation or law.

conservation: preservation, management, and care of natural and cultural resources.

constitution: an official document outlining the rules of a system or government.

conventions: agreements between countries, less formal than treaties.

decolonization: the act of granting a colony its independence.

delegates: individuals chosen to represent or act on behalf of an organization or government.

demographic: characteristics of a human population.

diplomatic: having to do with international negotiations without resorting to violence.

disarmament: the reduction of a nation's supply of weapons or strength of its armed forces.

due process: the official procedures in legal cases required by law to ensure that the rights of all people involves are protected.

embargo: a government order limiting or prohibiting trade.

envoys: diplomats who act on behalf of a national government.

epidemic: a widespread occurrence of an infectious disease.

ethnic cleansing: the killing or imprisonment of an ethnic minority by a dominant group.

exchange rates: rates at which money of one country is exchanged the money of another.

extradition: the handing over by one government of someone accused of a crime in a different country for trial or punishment.

extremist: having to do with radical political or religious beliefs.

factions: smaller groups within larger groups that have opposing ideas.

fascist: relating to a system of government characterized by dictatorship, repression of opposition, and extreme nationalism.

flashpoints: areas of intense conflict and insecurity that often erupt into violent confrontation.

forgery: the act of making or producing an illegal copy of something.

free-market economy: economic system in which businesses operate without government control in matters such as pricing and wage levels.

genocide: systematic killing of all people from a national, ethnic, or religious group, or an attempt to do so.

globalization: the various processes that increase connections peoples of the world.

gross domestic product: total value of all goods and services produced within a country.

guerrilla: unorganized and small-scale warfare carried out by independent units.

human trafficking: the practice of seizing people against their will for the purpose of "selling" them for work, usually in the sex trade.

humanitarian: being concerned with or wanting to promote the well-being of other humans.

ideological: based on a specific system of beliefs, values, and ideas forming the basis of a social, economic, or political philosophy

indigenous: relating to the original inhabitants of an area or environment.

infrastructure: physical structures of a region, made up of roads, bridges, and so forth.

isolationism: the belief that a country should limit their involvement in the affairs of other countries.

mandate: an official instruction by an authority.

mediation: the process of resolving a dispute.

money laundering: the transferring of illegally obtained money through various businesses and accounts so as to hide it.

nationalists: people with an extreme sense of loyalty to their country.

nationalize: takeover by a government of a private business.

pandemic: a widespread epidemic in which a disease spreads to many countries and regions of the world.

per capita income: average amount earned by each individual in a country.

preamble: introduction, or opening words of a document.

precedent: established practice; a decision used as the basis of future decisions.

proliferation: the rapid spread of something.

propaganda: information or publicity put out by an organization or government to spread and promote a policy or idea.

protocols: preliminary memoranda often formulated and signed by diplomatic negotiators.

rapporteur: an official in charge of investigating and reporting to an agency, institution, or other entity.

ratification: the act of formally approving something.

referendum: a vote of the entire electorate on a question or questions put before it by the government or similar body.

reparation: compensation made by a nation defeated by others in a war.

sanction: a punishment imposed as a result of breaking a rule or law.

signatories: persons or governments who have signed a treaty and are bound by it.

sovereignty: self-rule, usually of a nation.

standard of living: the minimum amount of necessities essential to maintaining a comfortable life.

summit: a meeting between heads of government or other high-ranking officials.

sustainable: able to be maintained so that the resource is not depleted or damaged.

veto: the power of a person, country, or branch of government to reject the legislation of another.

INDEX

PICTURE CREDITS

BIOGRAPHIES

Author

HEATHER DOCALAVICH first became interested in the work of the United Nations while working as an adviser for a high school Model UN program. She lives in Hilton Head Island, South Carolina, with her four children.

Series Advisor

BRUCE RUSSETT is Dean Acheson Professor of Political Science at Yale University and editor of the Journal of Conflict Resolution. He has taught or researched at Columbia, Harvard, M.I.T., Michigan, and North Carolina in the United States, and educational institutions in Belgium, Britain, Israel, Japan, and the Netherlands. He has been president of the International Studies Association and the Peace Science Society, and holds an honorary doctorate from Uppsala University in Sweden. He was principal adviser to the U.S. Catholic Bishops for their pastoral letter on nuclear deterrence in 1985, and codirected the staff for the 1995 Ford Foundation report, *The United Nations in Its Second Half Century*. He has served as editor of the *Journal of Conflict Resolution* since 1973. The twenty-five books he has published include *The Once and Future Security Council* (1997), *Triangulating Peace: Democracy, Interdependence, and International Organizations* (2001), *World Politics: The Menu for Choice* (8th edition 2006), and *Purpose and Policy in the Global Community* (2006).